Life's Magical Meanings

by Wayne Lee

Original Artwork by
Cheryl Paige Bozarth

Wayne Lee Enterprises Inc.
Box 75161, Edmonton, Alberta, Canada T6E 6K1
Telephone (780) 989-7000 or 1-866-306-7111
Email: admin@waynelee.com
www.waynelee.com

Library and Archives Canada Cataloguing in Publication

Lee, Wayne, 1969 -
Life's magical meanings / by Wayne Lee; original artwork by Cheryl Paige Bozarth.

ISBN 0-9735675-0-3

1. Acronyms. 2. Inspiration. I. Bozarth, Cheryl Paige II. Title.

PE1693.L43 2004 423'.15 C2004-904155-X

Printed in China June 2009

Acknowledgements

I wish to thank all of my friends, family and personal success team who have supported me and continue to support me in achieving my life long dreams. A warm thanks goes to Shirley Casavant, Grant Steele, Tamara Eder and Ronda Petersen who helped format and give this project life. I owe a heartfelt thanks to Cheryl Paige Bozarth and her artistic genius. She has made this project absolute magic.

About the Author

Wayne Lee

Wayne Lee is a former five time Canadian amateur wrestling champion and schoolteacher who had an unrelenting passion for entertaining and empowering people. He took a childhood interest in magic and a fascination with visualization and transformed himself from classroom instructor to Canada's Crown Prince of Entertainment and Empowerment. Wayne found a new way to educate people about the power of the mind and spread his philosophy that *"laughter is the best medicine"*.

Over the years, Wayne has used hypnosis to excite, entertain and mesmerize thousands of audiences across North America. He has performed over 2000 shows, hypnotizing over 20,000 people to explore the limits of their imagination.

As well as entertaining, Wayne educates and empowers audiences with his *Life is Magic* Motivational Presentations. He teaches people how to magically create more health, wealth and happiness in their lives.

Wayne's other projects include his award-winning feature length documentary, *The Deeper You Go* and his first book, *Secrets of Success for Magicians and Stage Hypnotists*. *The Deeper You Go* chronicles the metamorphosis of Wayne's hilarious hypnosis stage show into a Life is Magic seminar encouraging people to discover all of their dreams, goals and aspirations.

Whether an audience engages in Wayne's hypnosis performance or his powerful presentations, the results are always exciting, entertaining, empowering and something they will never forget.

ARTIST CHERYL PAIGE BOZARTH brings her passion for art and nature together through her exotic wildlife pieces, dramatic landscape series and vibrant abstract color studies. Each painting is a direct reflection of her interpretations and observations of the natural world, celebrating its capacity to convey universal concepts of speed, grace, love, happiness and even hostility.

Her paintings help establish a sense of place, a desirable feeling amidst the clutter and confusion of today's society. The subjects of her paintings vary dramatically; a tribute to the diversity of experience that is essential to life.

Originally from Sexsmith, Alberta, Cheryl holds a degree in Environmental Management. Having travelled extensively throughout the National Parks of Canada, the USA and Latin America, she departed from her career in Urban Planning to express her interpretations of nature into contemporary art and design.

Cheryl's works can be found in numerous private and corporate collections. In the past year she has showcased throughout much of Western Canada and through numerous community-based projects and exhibits.

The artwork featured in this book is available as paintings or prints, and can be purchased by contacting the artist at www.cpaigedesign.com.

ABOUT THE ARTIST

Cheryl Paige Bozarth

THE PATH I HAVE TAKEN to develop the magical meanings found in this book has been fascinating. I have realized that the words we use every day determine how we think, feel, and act. Words are magical symbols allowing us to connect with ourselves and with other people. Even though words are powerful, they are only as powerful as the meanings we attach to them. It is not the words that matter, but the connections the words imply.

From a deep desire and inner guidance, I needed to make words more meaningful in my life, so I began creating acronyms from words. Developing my first acronym was a synchronistic and profound experience. It was May 9, 2002, and my crew and I were returning home to Edmonton, Alberta from a hypnosis performance in Quill Lake, Saskatchewan. I had an overwhelming urge to develop a representation or acronym for the word FOCUS, because I believe having focus is what life is all about. Within five minutes it came to me… Fixed Ongoing Concentration, Unlimited Success. My crew member, Corey, said the acronym was brilliant! Within seconds my vehicle began to vibrate. I pulled the motorhome onto the side of the barren Saskatchewan highway and quickly looked at the gas gauge. Realizing we had run out of gas, Corey and I began to laugh about the situation. We had forgotten to 'focus' on the fact that we would need plenty of gas to travel such a long distance. We had overlooked the importance of 'Fixed Ongoing Concentration, Unlimited Success.' This experience taught me to always remember the important things in life, so that I don't ever 'run out of gas.' From that day forward, I have had the divine guidance to develop hundreds of acronyms that have helped to make my life more meaningful.

During an unexpected and synchronistic encounter last year, I met a talented and gifted local artist – Cheryl Paige Bozarth. Upon seeing the brilliance of her works, I asked Cheryl if she would use her talents to create a painting for each of my acronyms. Cheryl agreed to paint the *Life's Magical Meanings* series – the paintings represent the acronyms presented in this book. I am honoured to showcase Cheryl's remarkable work in this manner.

BY SHARING LIFE'S MAGICAL MEANINGS WITH YOU, IT IS MY SINCERE GOAL THAT YOU WILL DISCOVER AND APPRECIATE THE MAGIC THAT EXISTS IN YOUR LIFE.

Magical Meanings CONTENTS

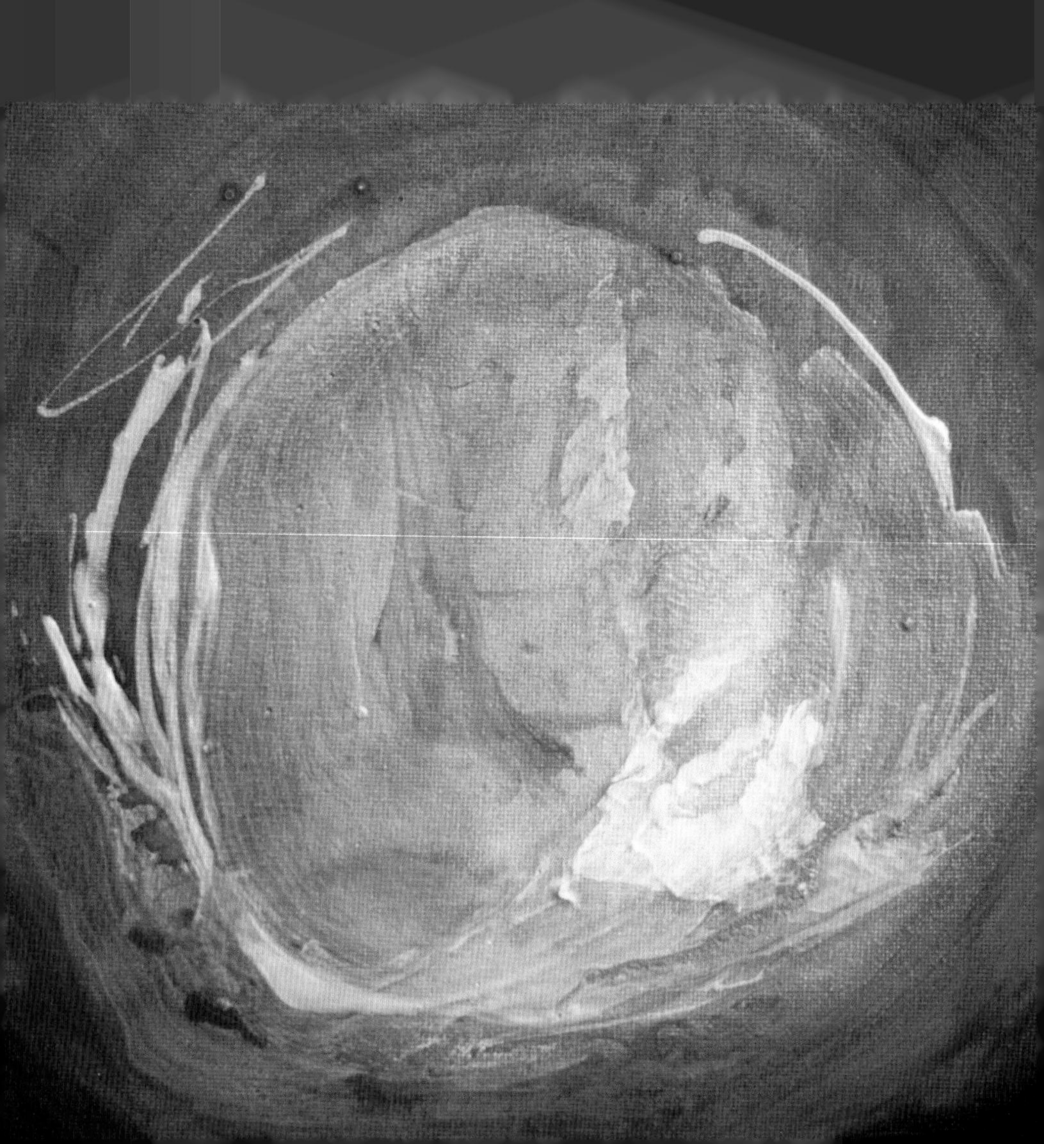

A

Natural

Guardian

Expressing

Love

BRILLIANT

ESSENCE

AND

UNLIMITED

TO

YOU

Beauty

BELIEF

BOUNDLESS

ENERGY

LED

INTO

EXPRESSING

FACT

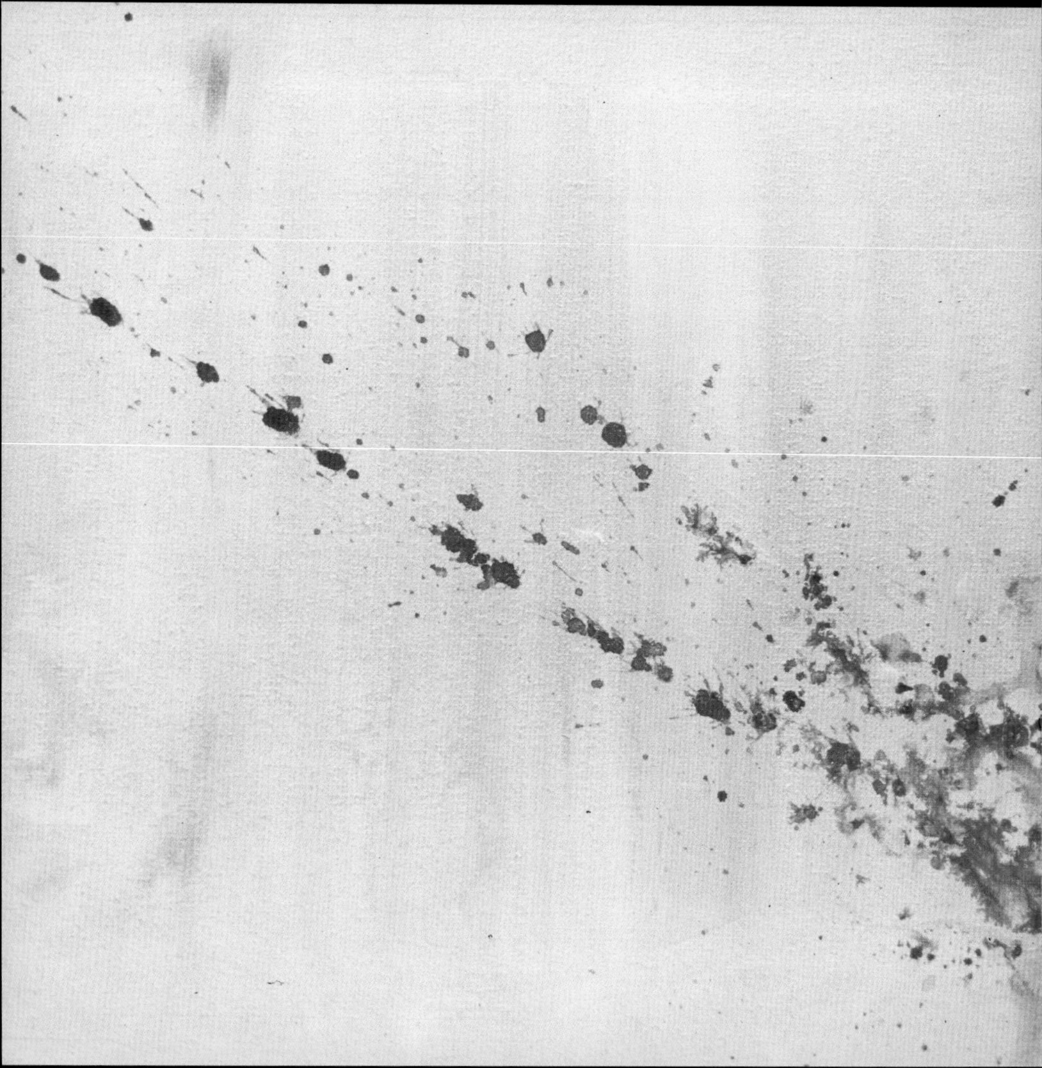

Beauty,

Love,

Intention,

Strength,

Serenity

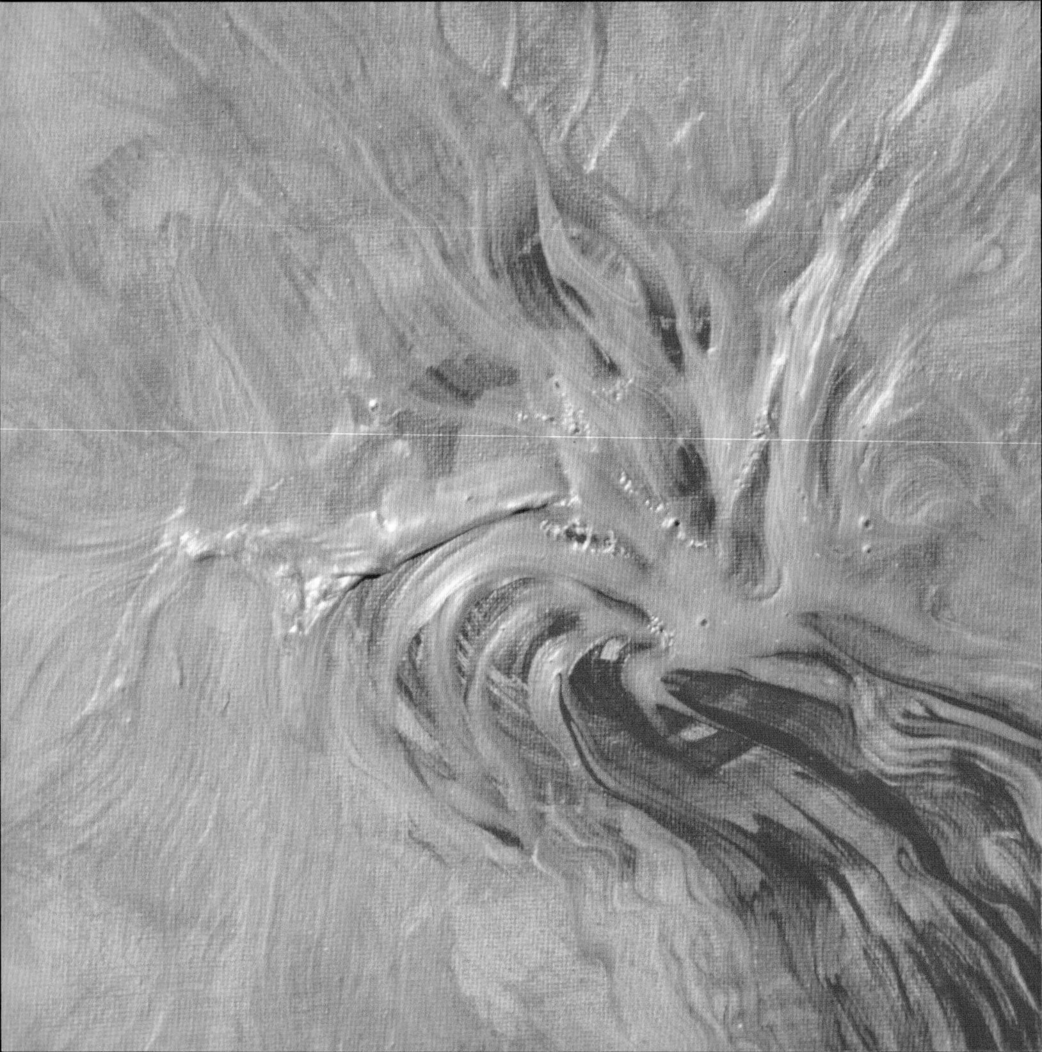

BEAUTIFUL

OUTSTANDING

DYNAMIC

YOU

CALM

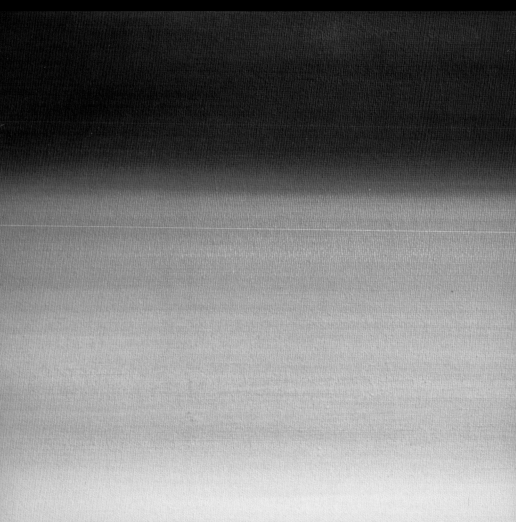

Come All, Let's Meditate

CARE

Compassion

And

Real

Empathy

Care

CHOICES

CREATE

HABITS,

OPPORTUNITIES,

INFLUENCES,

CONSEQUENCES,

EXPERIENCES,

SUCCESSES

CONNECT

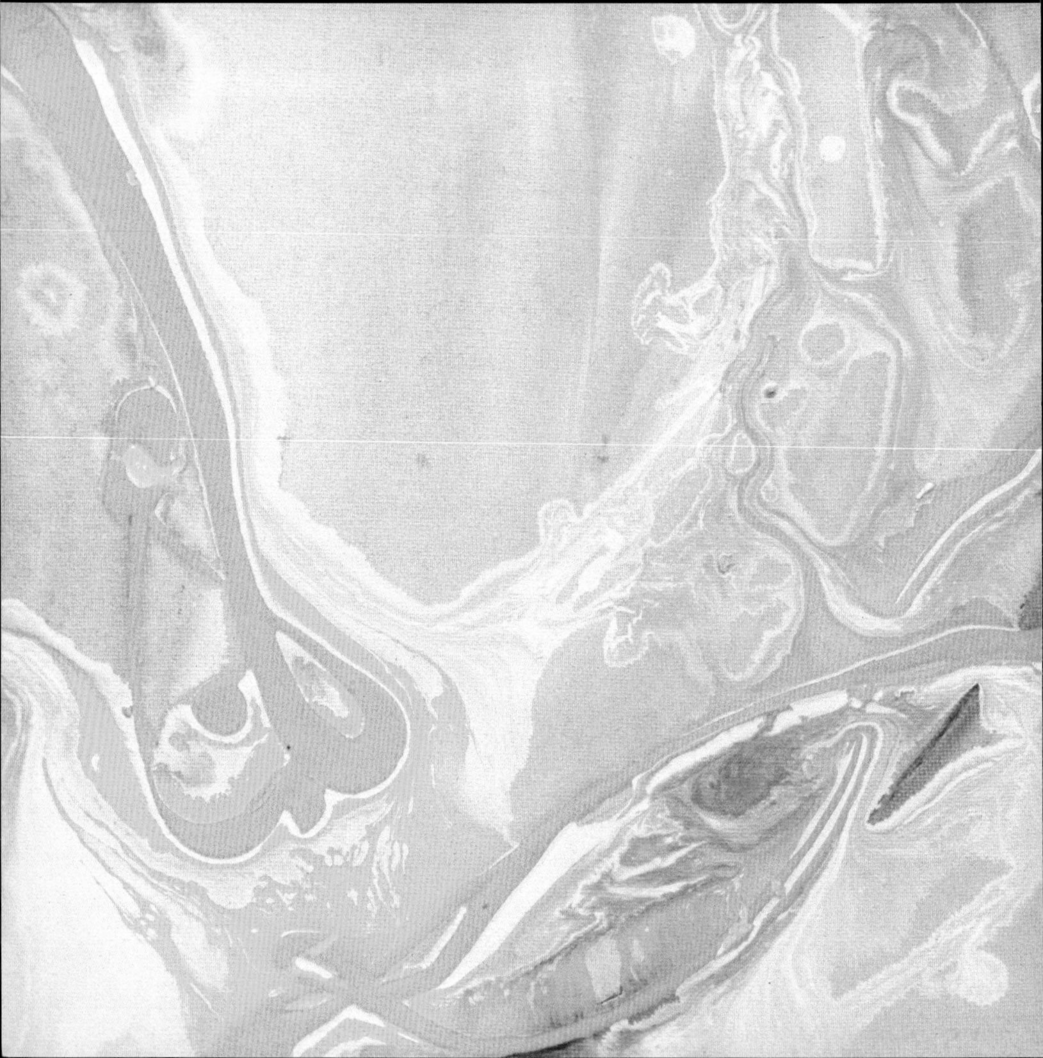

COMMUNICATING

ONENESS,

NETWORKING

NATURALLY,

EVERYONE

COMING

TOGETHER

Connect

CHOICE

RELEASING

EXPRESSION

AND

TRANSFORMING

ENERGY

Dynamic

And

Natural

Creative

Expression

DEFINITE

EXPRESSIVE

CHOICE

IN

DIRECTING

ENERGY

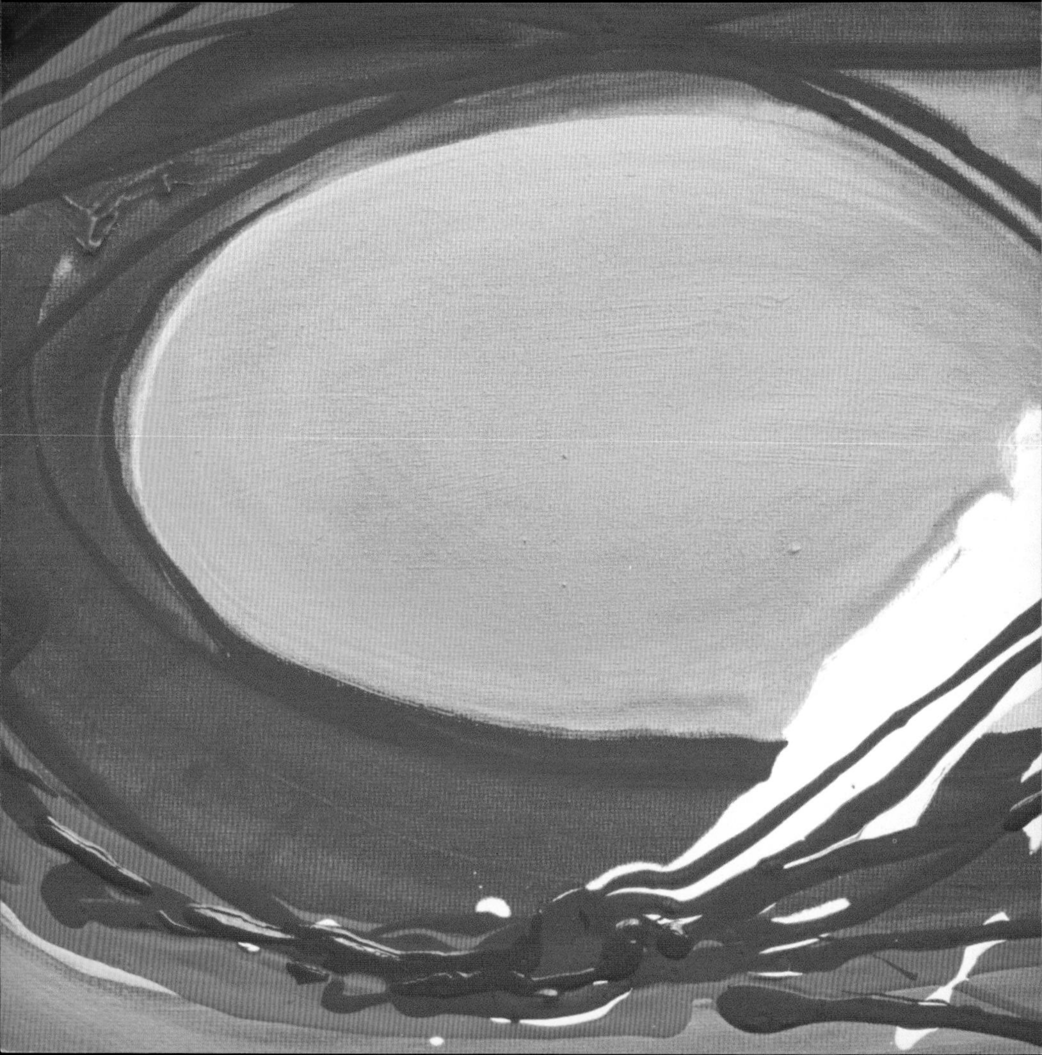

DIRECTS

ENERGY

STRONGLY

INTO

REAL

EXPRESSION

DREAM

Desires

Realized,

Expected

And

Made

EXISTS

NATURALLY,

ETERNALLY,

RELEASES

GREAT

YEARNING

FAITH

FEELING

AND

IMAGINING

THINGS

HAPPENING

FEEL

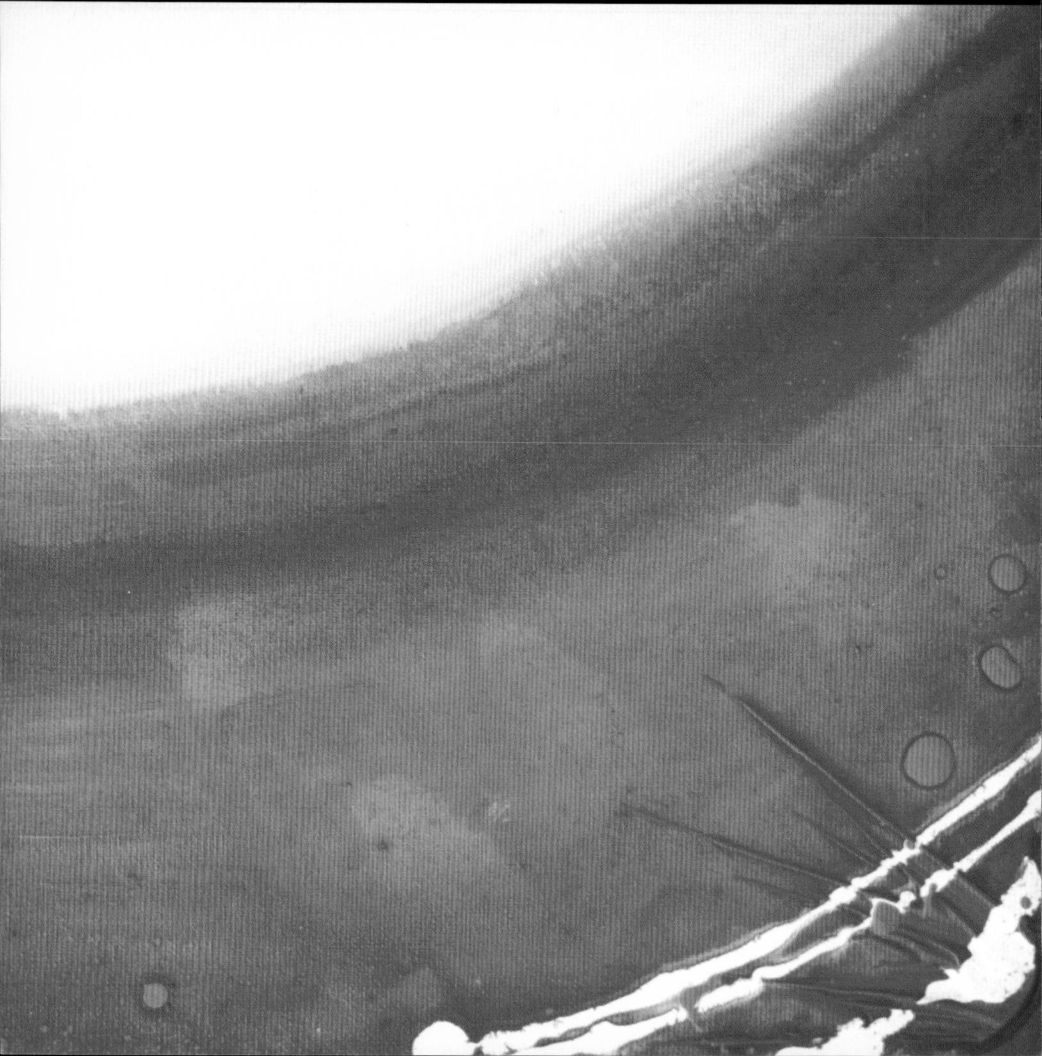

FLOWING

EMOTIONS

EXPRESSING

LIFE

FLOW

Fluid Living, Outstanding Work

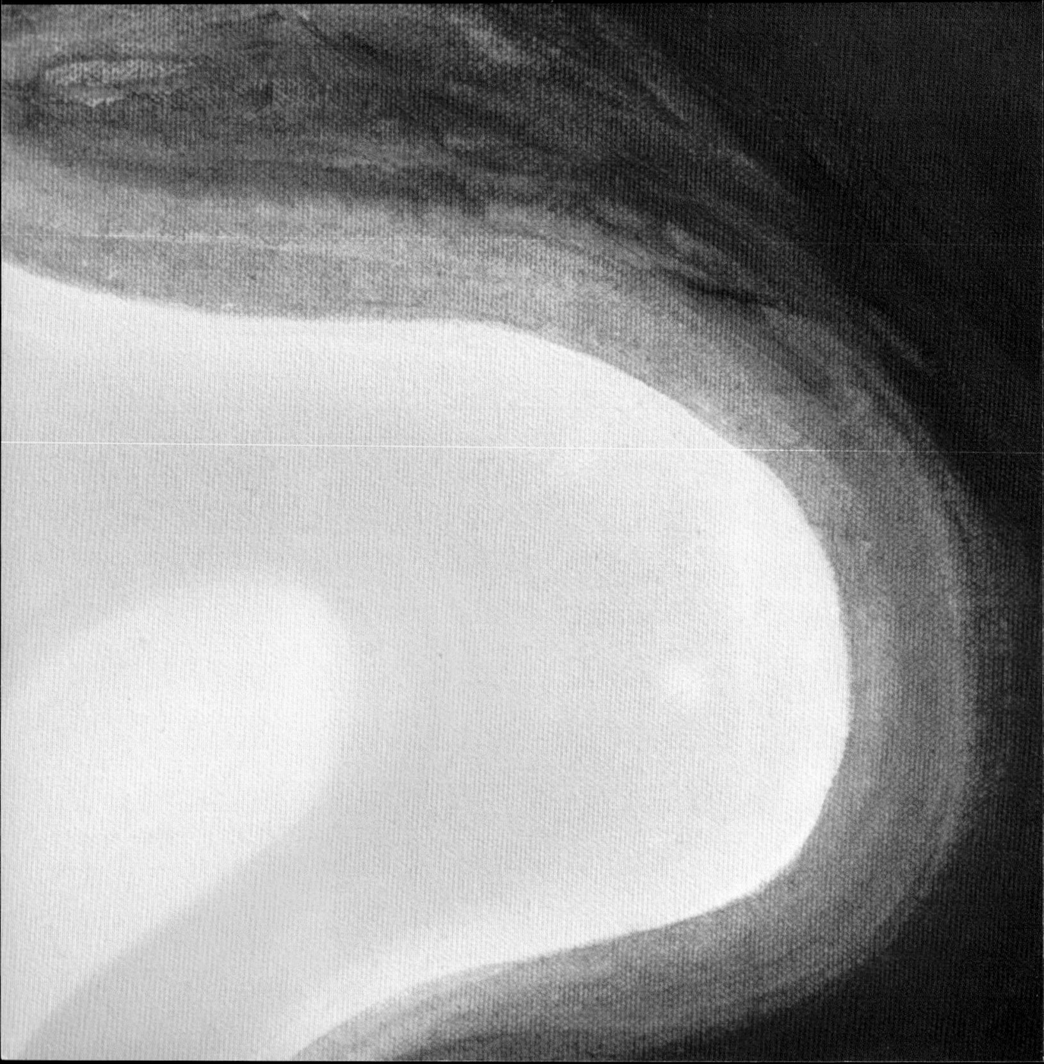

FIXED

ONGOING

CONCENTRATION,

UNLIMITED

SUCCESS

Feeling Utopia Now

Generosity In Various Expressions

GOAL

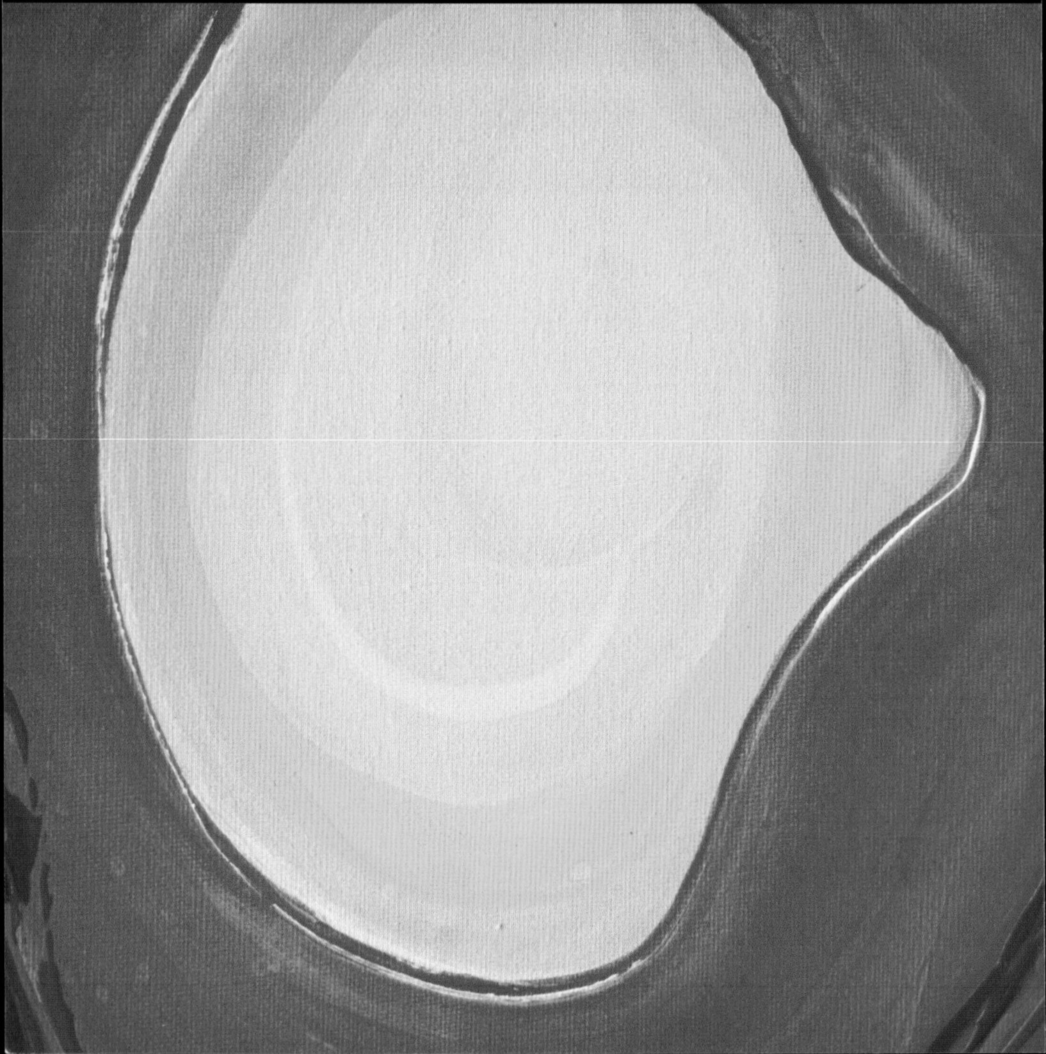

GREAT

ORGANIZED

ACHIEVABLE

LOVE

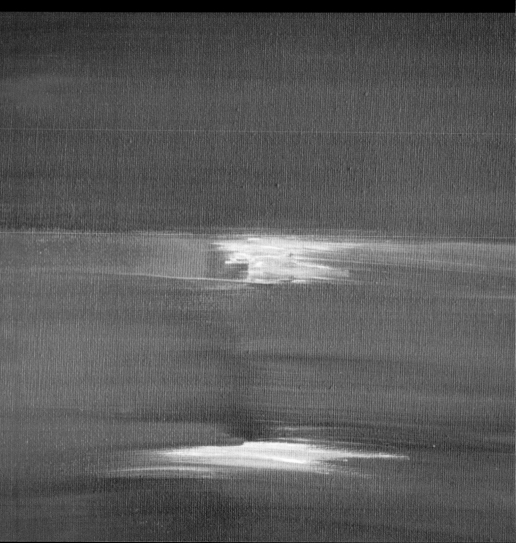

HAVING
A
BELIEF
INGRAINED
TOTALLY

HAVING
A
BEHAVIOUR
INGRAINED
TOTALLY

Heart

Ascending

Real

Music

Onto

Navigating

Yourself

Harmony

HEAL

HARMONIOUS

ENERGY

ALLOWING

LIFE

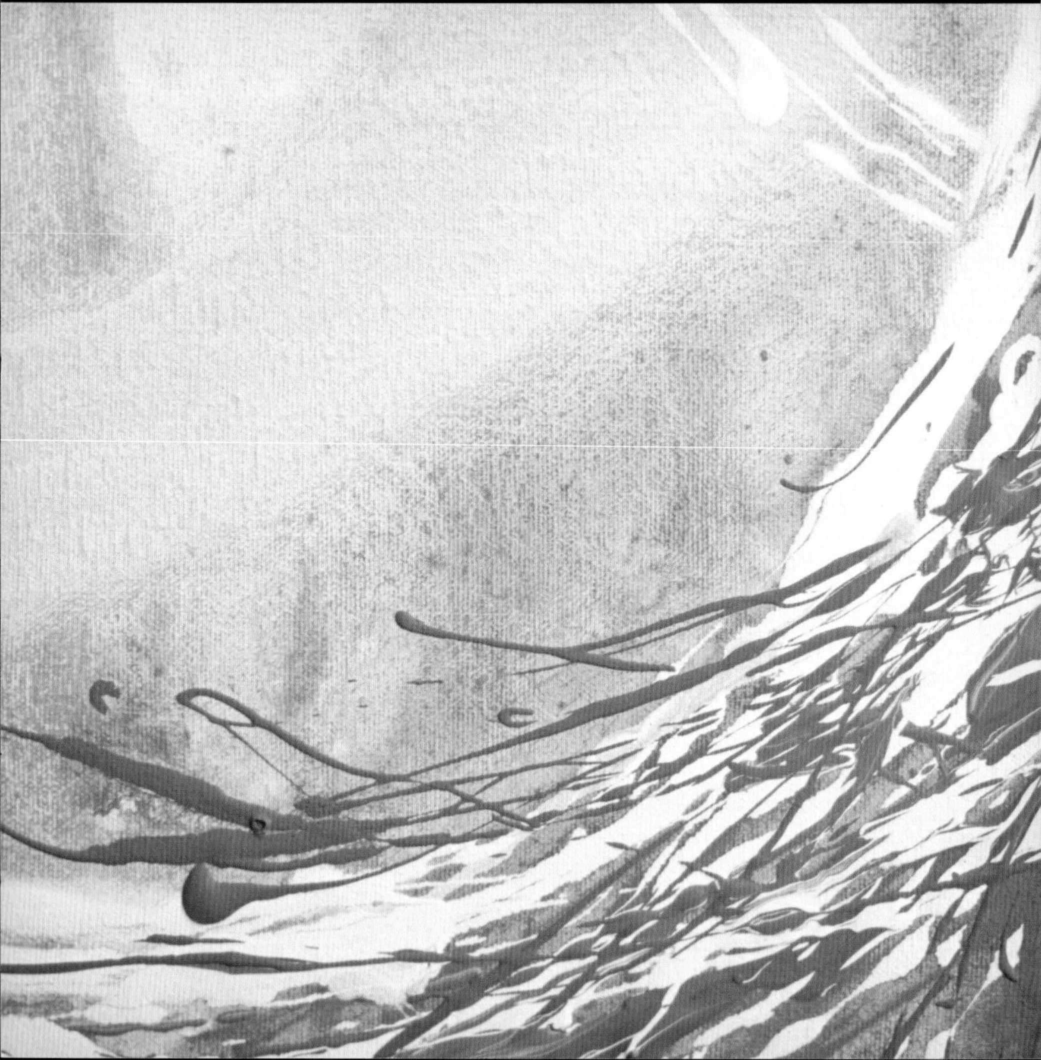

HARMONIOUS

ENERGY

ALLOWING

LIFE

TO

HAPPEN

HEART

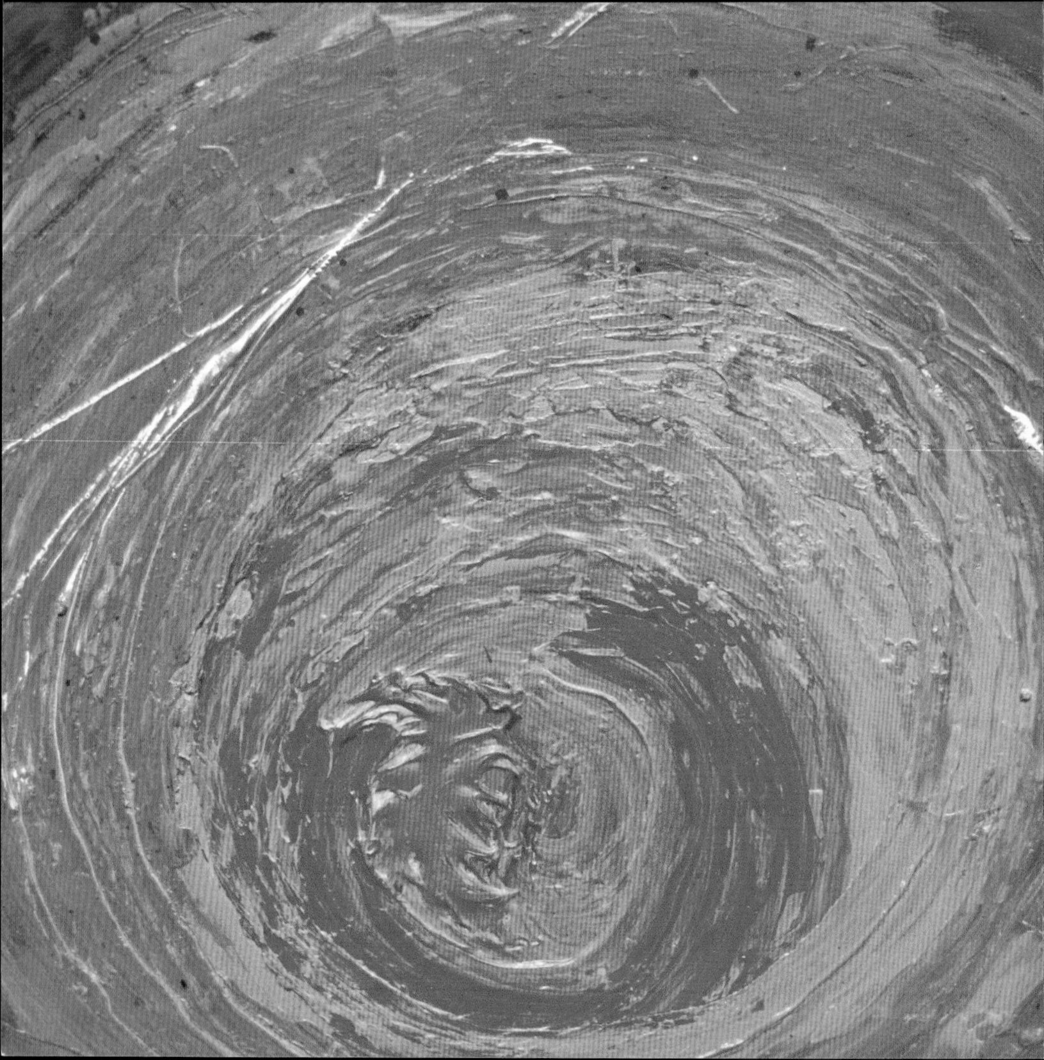

HARMONIOUS

ESSENCE

AND

REAL

TRUTH

HARMONIOUS

EXISTENCE

AND

VIVIDLY

EXPERIENCED

NOW

Heaven

HARMONIOUS

ENERGY

LIFTING

PEOPLE

HONEST

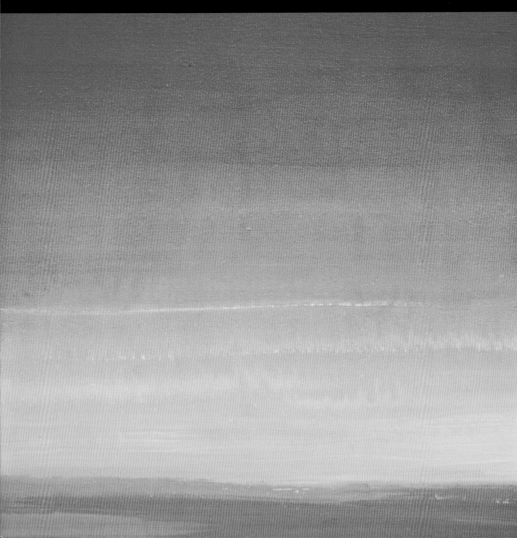

HAVING

OPENNESS,

NATURALLY

EXPRESSING

SELF

TRUTH

HOPE

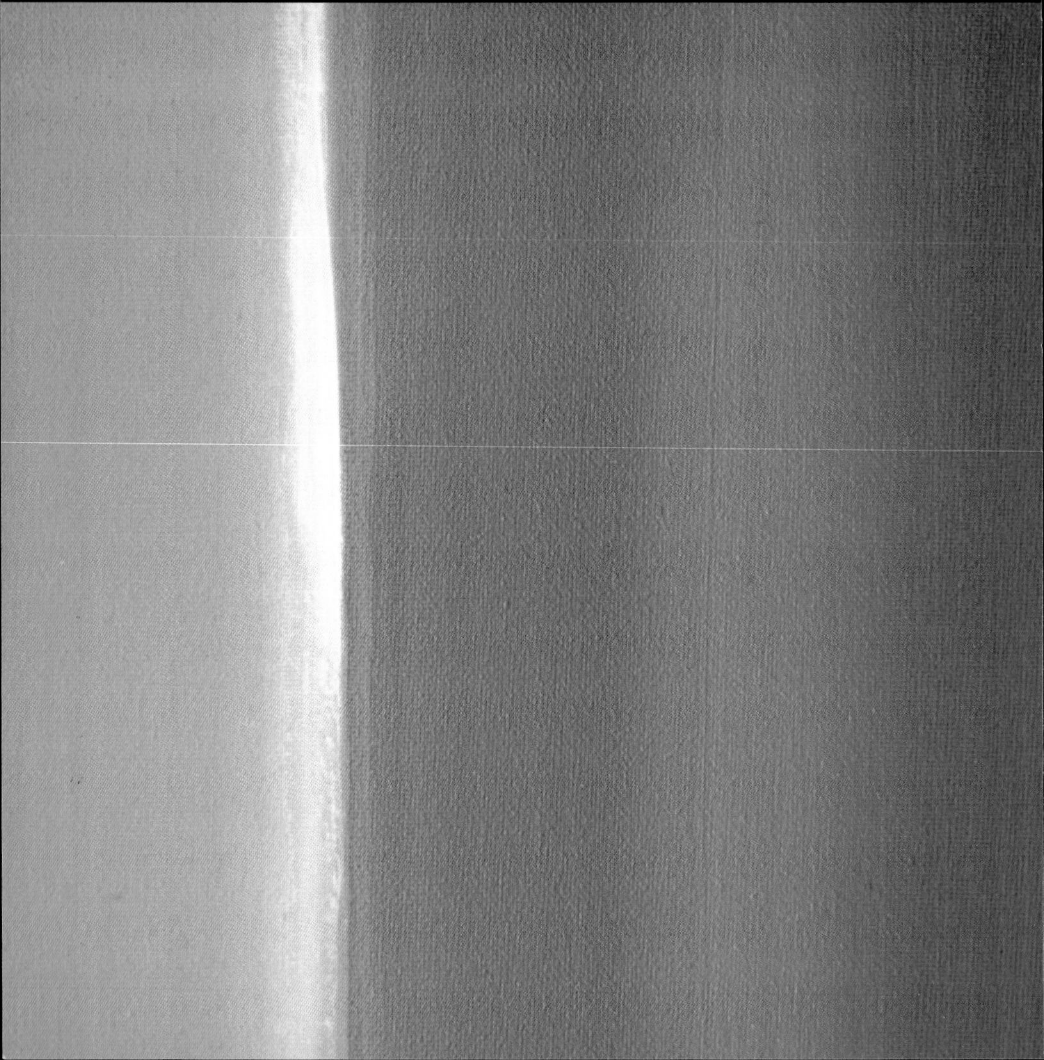

HAVING

OPPORTUNITIES,

POSSIBILITIES

EXPECTED

Hope

HUG

HARMONIOUS

UNCONDITIONAL

GIFT

Hug

IMAGINE

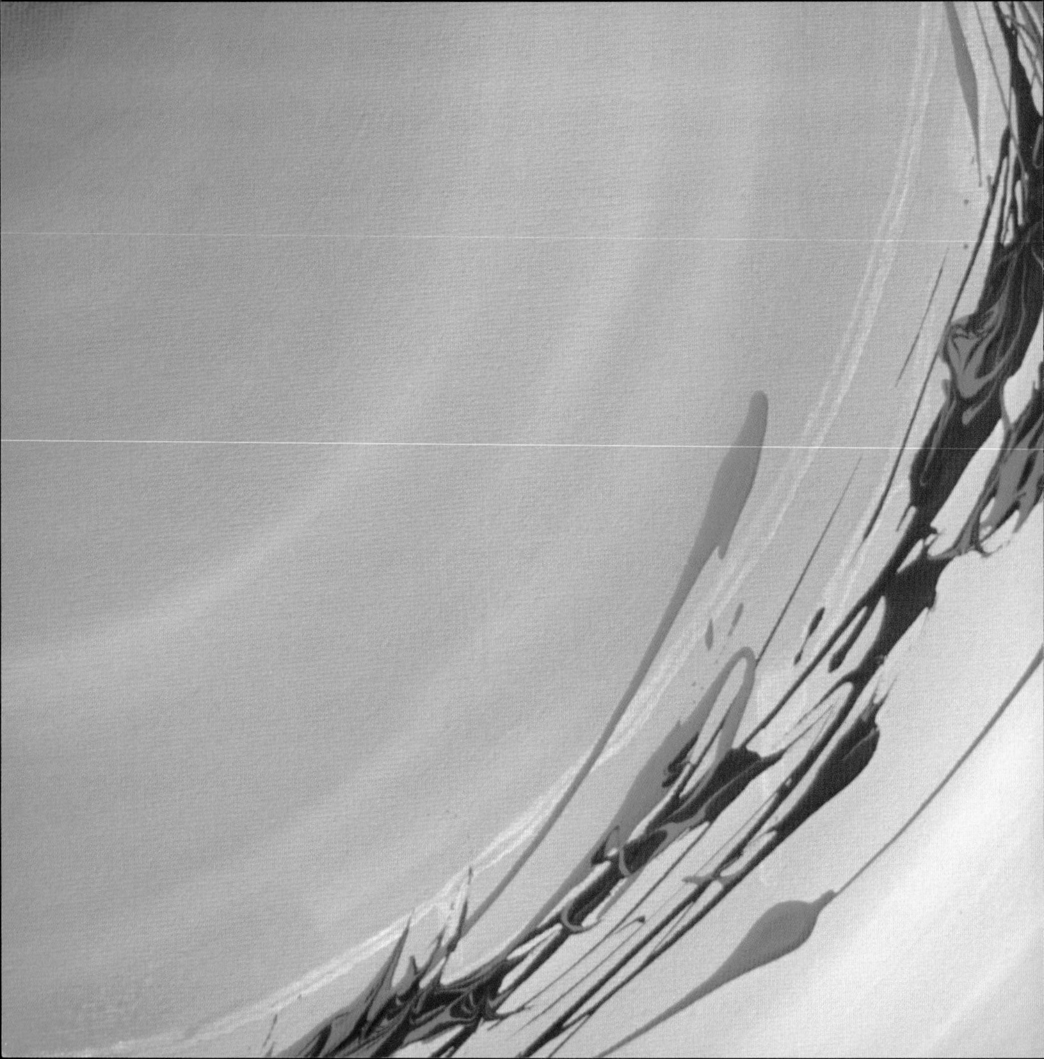

IDEAS

MANIFESTING

AND

GROWING

INTO

NATURAL

EXISTENCE

JOY

Jewel Of You

Joy

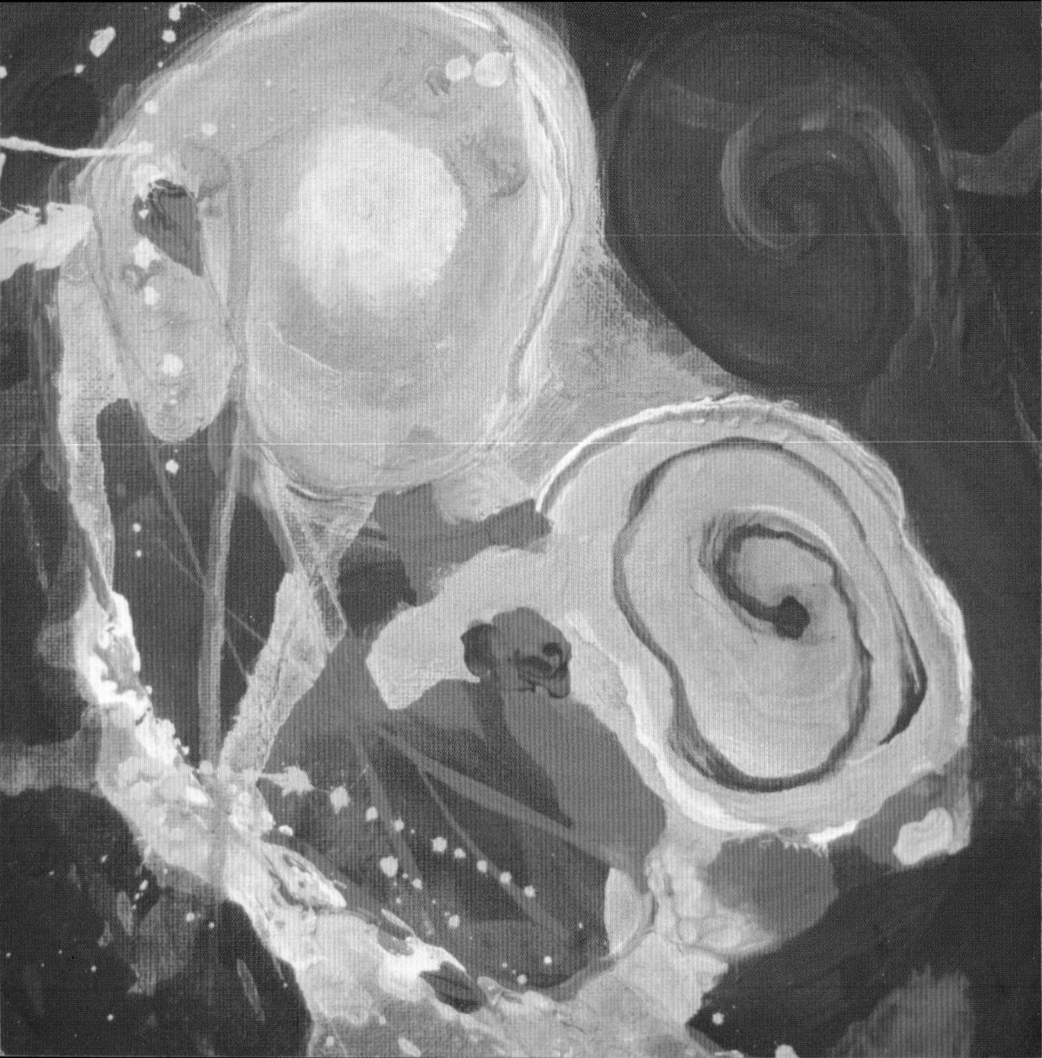

LIVING

AND

USING

GREAT

HUMOUR

LEARN,

EXPERIENCE,

AND

DIRECT

LEARN

Listen,

Experience,

And

Realize

Now

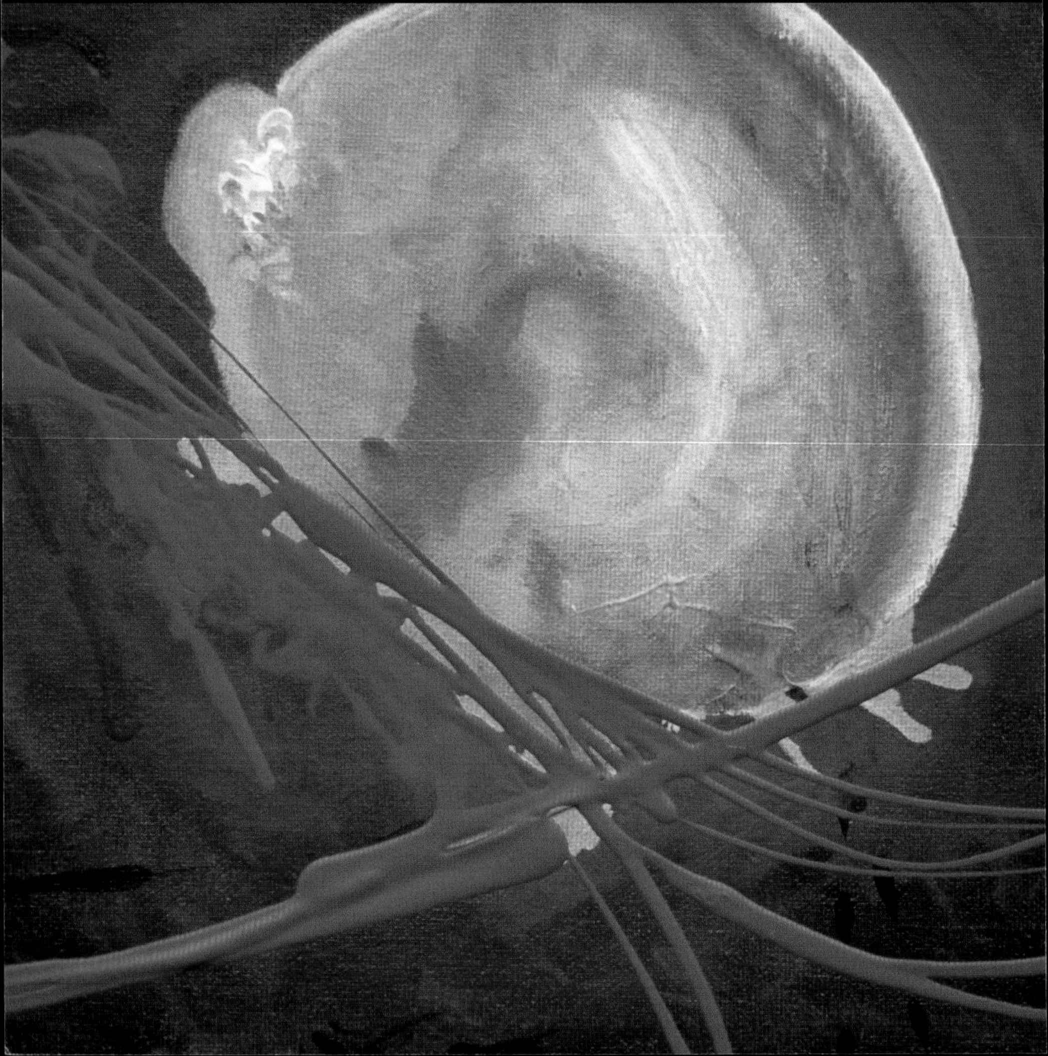

Love

In

Full

Expression

LIVE

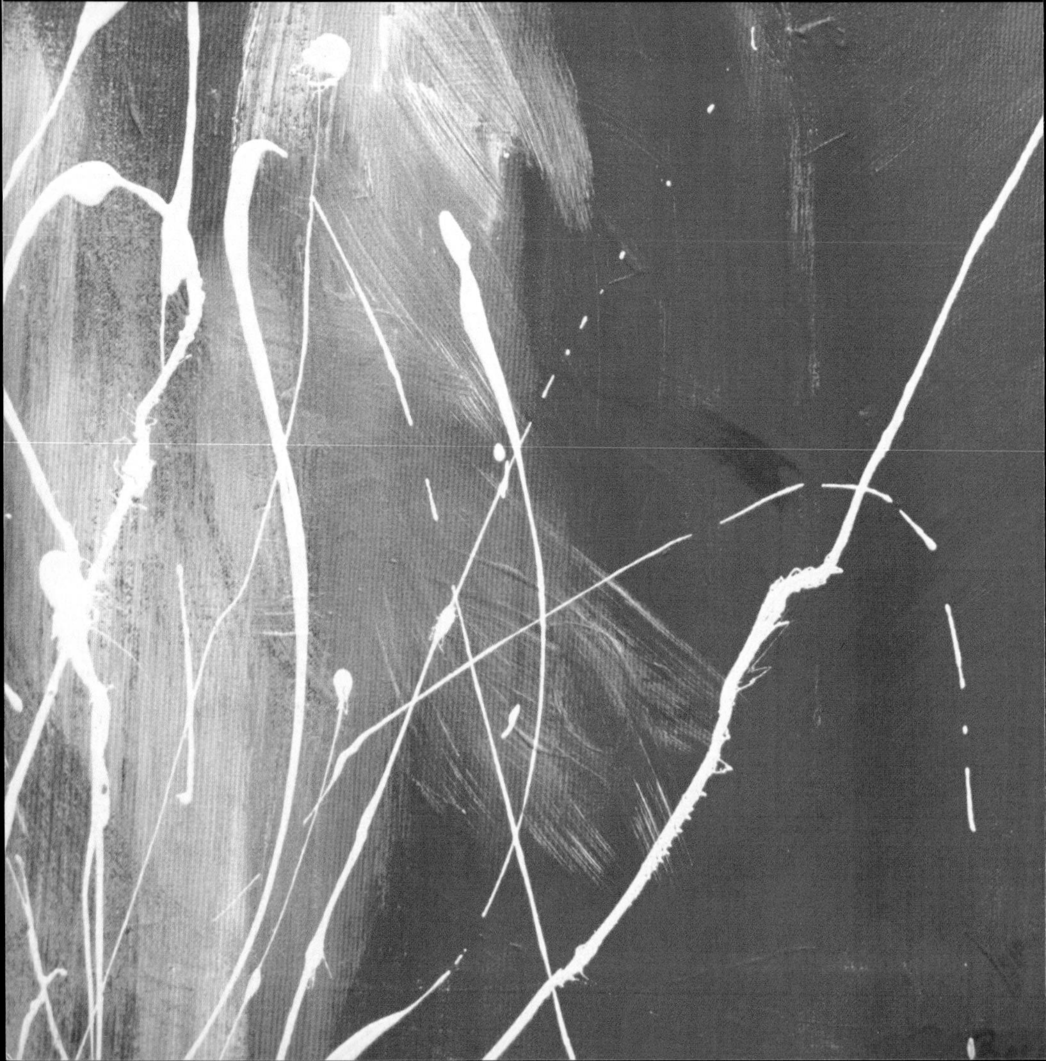

Love

In

Various

Expressions

LOVE

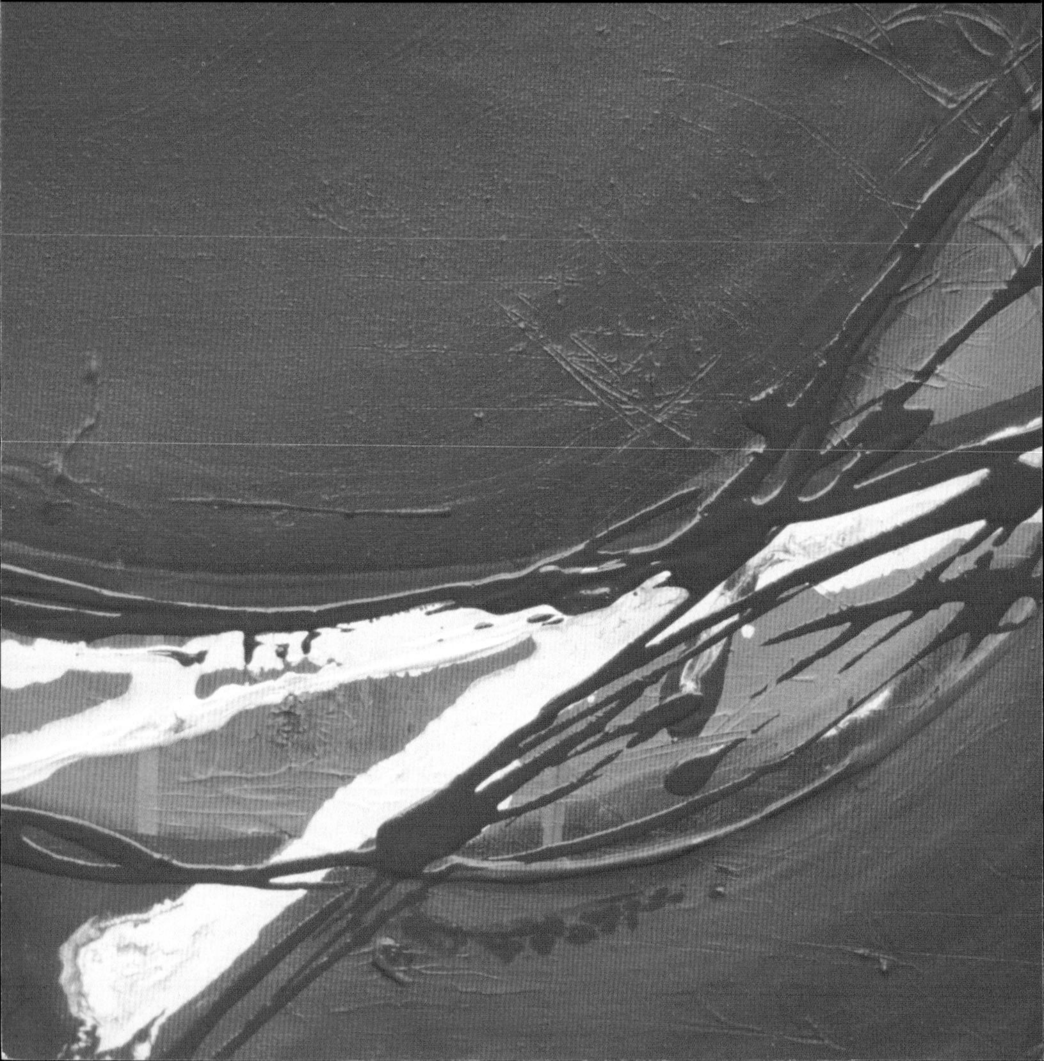

LIFE'S

ONE

VALUABLE

EXPRESSION

MANIFEST

AND

GROW

INTO

CREATION

MEMORY

MIND

EXPERIENCING

MOMENTS

OF

RELIVING

YOURSELF

MIND

MASSIVE

INTELLIGENT

NAVIGATION

DEVICE

MIRROR

OF

NATURALLY

EXPRESSING

YOURSELF

MUSIC

MELODIES

UNIQUELY

STIMULATING

INNER

CREATIVITY

NOW

NEVER

ON

WAIT

PASSION

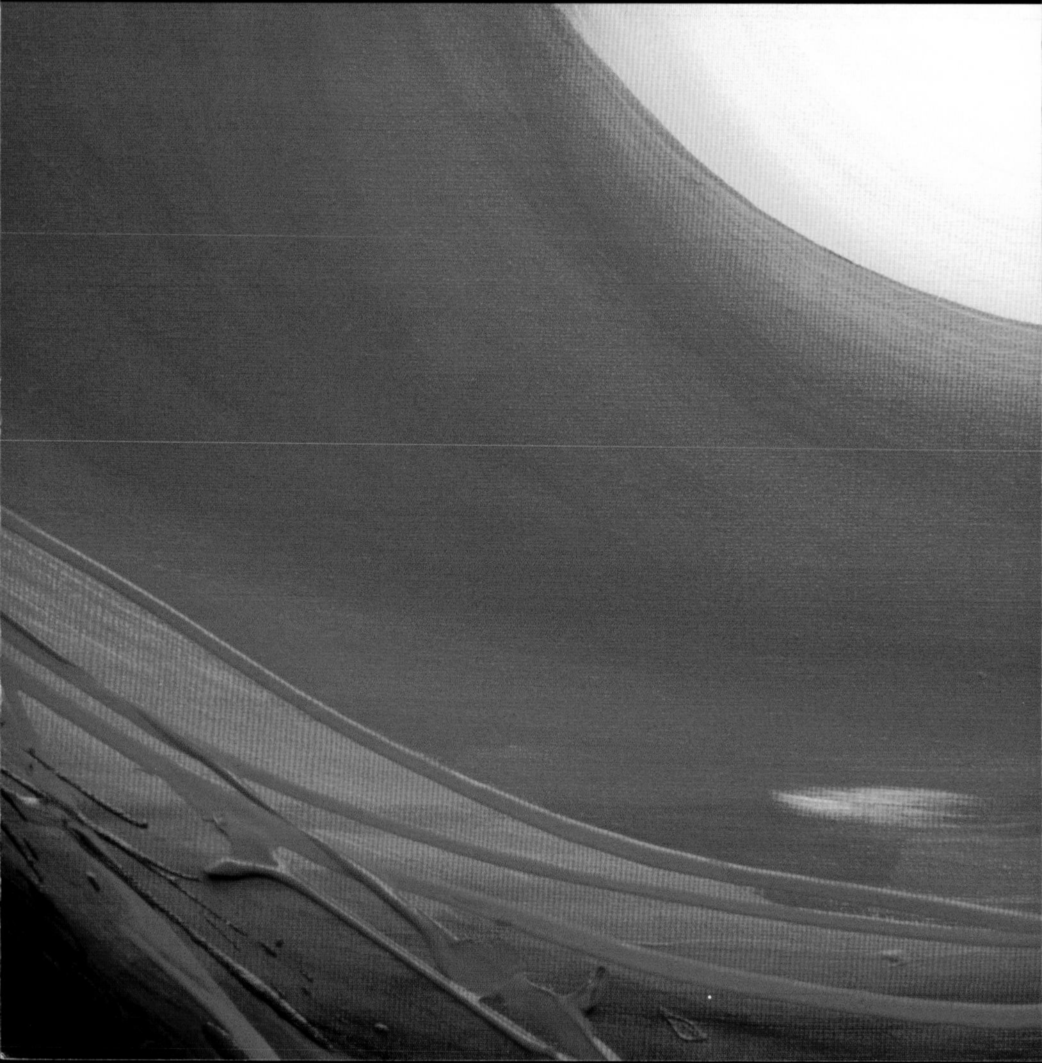

PROJECTS

A

STRONG

SENSATION

INTO

ONGOING

NAVIGATION

P E A C E

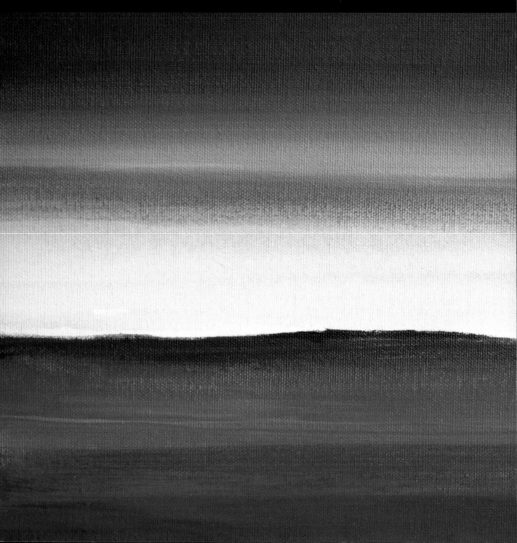

PROFOUND

EXPRESSION

AND

CALM

EXISTENCE

Peace

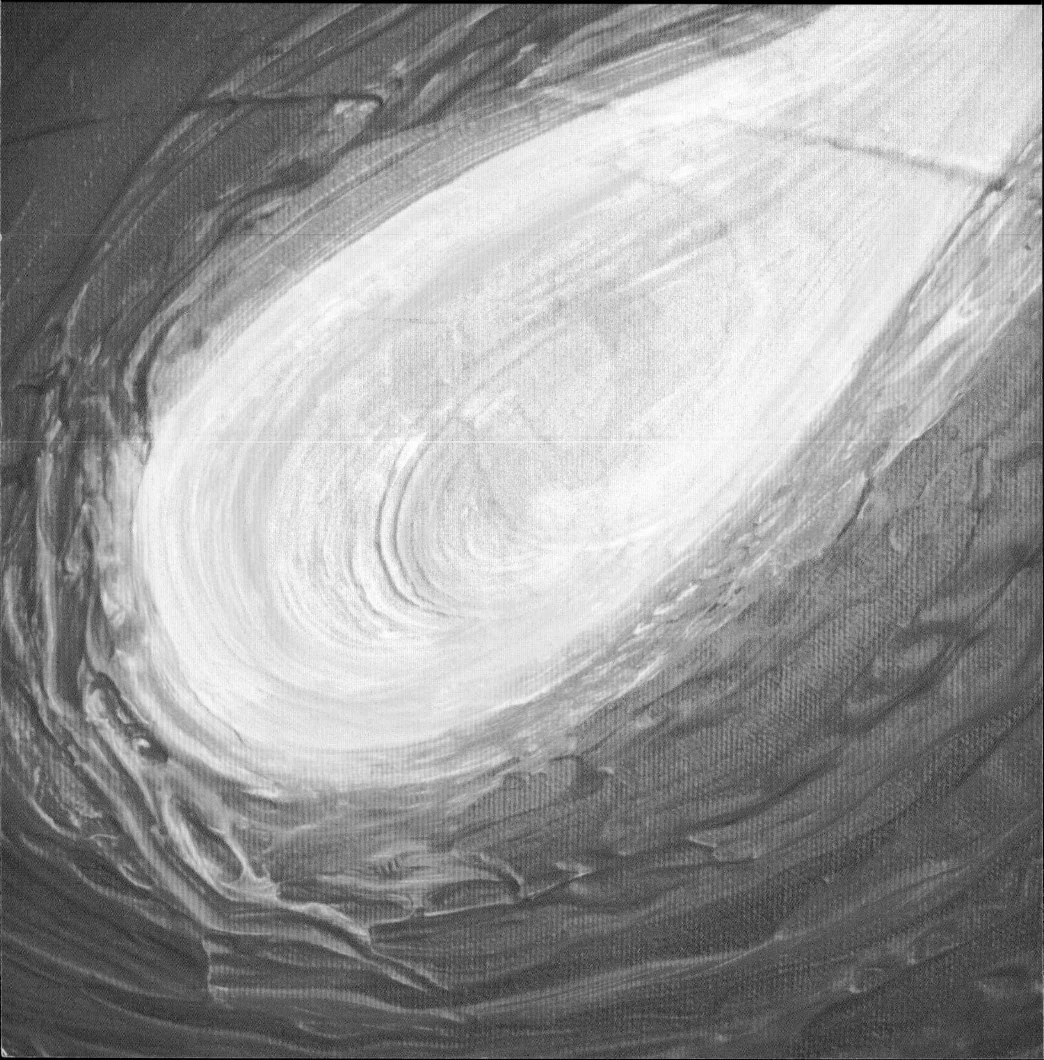

POTENTIAL

OUTSTANDING

WORK

EXPERIENCED

REAL

REAL

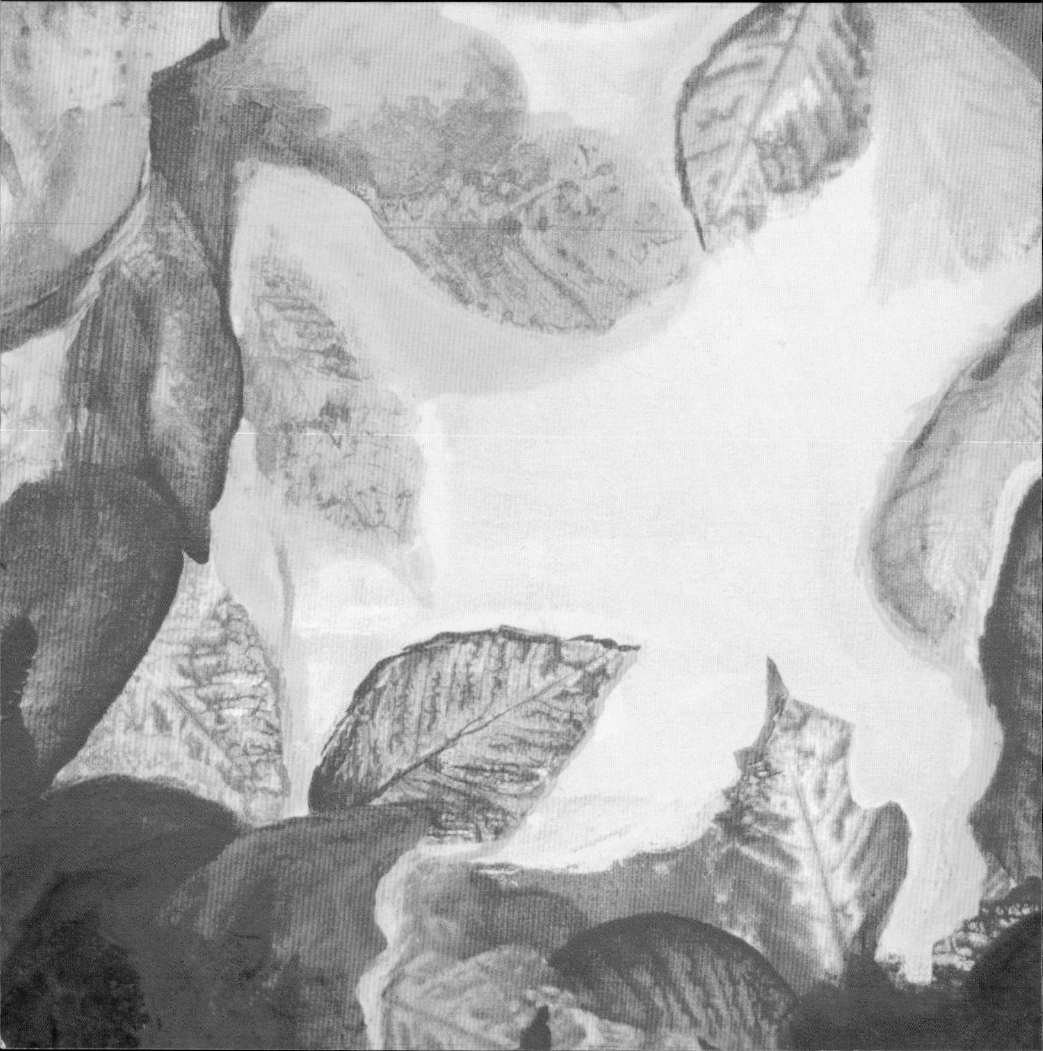

REFLECTS

EVERYTHING

ABOUT

LIFE

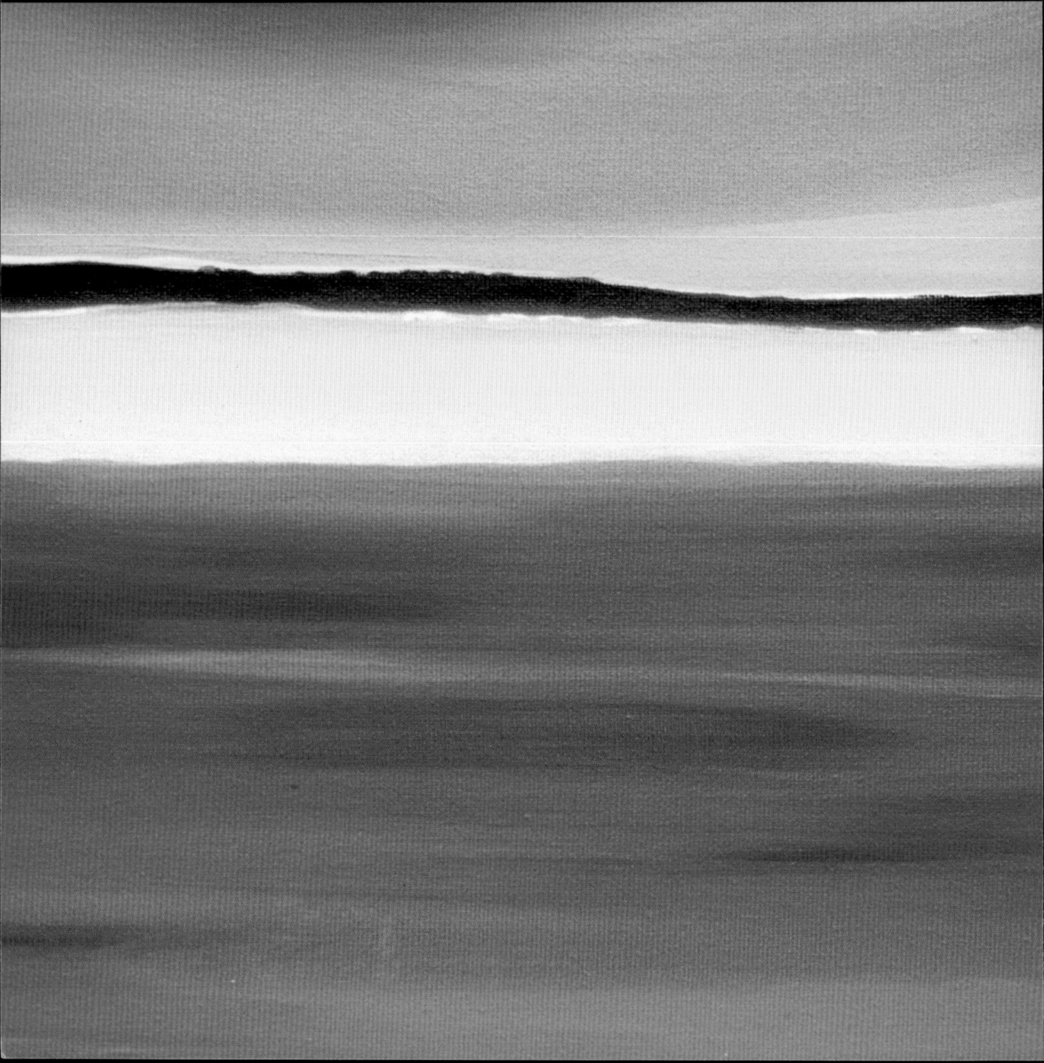

Release

Energy

Loosely

And

Xhale

SERVE

SENDING

EVERYONE

REALLY

VALUABLE

ENERGY

Source

Energy

Xpressed

SMILE

SIMPLE

MOVEMENT

INCORPORATING

LIFTING

EVERYONE

Smile

SOUL

SOURCE
OF
UNIQUE
LIFE

SOURCE
OF
UNITING
LIFE

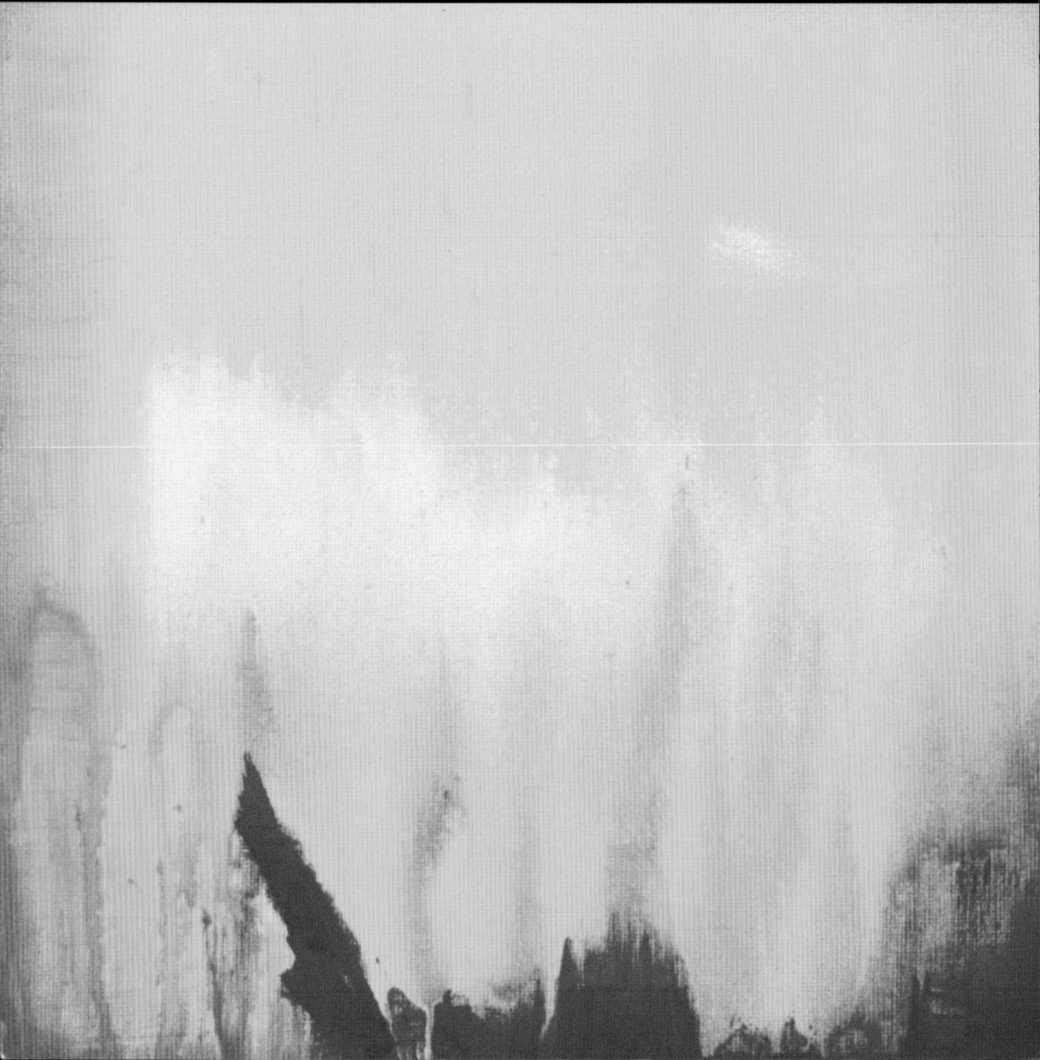

SOURCE

POWER

INSIDE

RESONATING

INFINITE

TRUTH

SIMPLY

USING

CONCENTRATION,

CONFIDENCE,

EFFORT,

SKILLS,

SELF-DESIRES

To

Express

And

Convey

Harmony

Tool
In
Measuring
Eternity

TRUST

TO

REALLY

UNDERSTAND

SELF

TRUTH

Trust

TRUTH

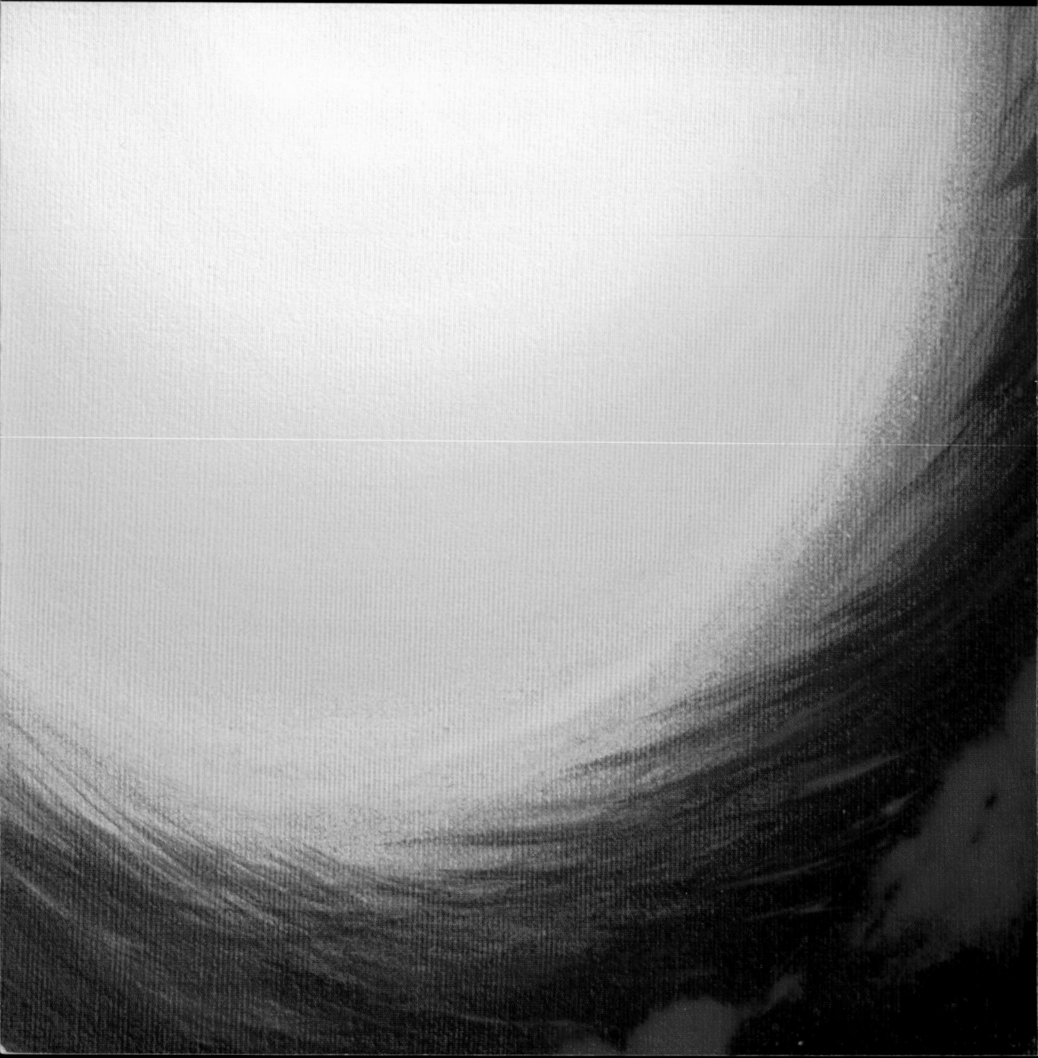

To

Really

Understand

The

Heart

VIVID

IMAGES

STIMULATING

INDIVIDUAL

ONGOING

NAVIGATION

WEALTH

Welcoming

Endless

Abundance,

Living

To

Have

Wealth

Reflections...

"Words are like planets, each with its own gravitational pull." ~ Kenneth Burke

"Seek always for the best words and the happiest expressions you can find." ~ Lord Chesterfield

"Words... are a kind of natural resource, it is impossible to have too many of them." ~ Robert Claiborne

"Every word was once a poem." ~ Ralph Waldo Emerson

"A word is not crystal, transparent and unchanging. It is the skin of living thought." ~ Oliver Wendell Homes, Jr.

"Words, like eyeglasses, obscure everything they do not make clear." ~ Joseph Joubert

"Words are, of course, the most powerful drug used by mankind." ~ Rudyard Kipling

"Words, like flowers, have their colours too." ~ Ernest Rhys

"Language is the memory of the human race." ~ William Henry Smith

"Uttering a word is like striking a note on the keyboard of the imagination." ~ Ludwig Wittgenstein